S0-BBT-131

LANGUAGE ARTS FOLDER FUN

Activities For Reinforcement And Enrichment

by Kathy Blankenhorn
and
Joanne Richards

Incentive Publications, Inc.
Nashville, Tennessee

Illustrated by Gayle Seaberg Harvey
Cover by Terrence Donaldson
Edited by Leslie Britt

ISBN 0-86530-316-9

Copyright ©1995 by Incentive Publications, Inc., Nashville, TN. All rights reserved. No part of this publication may be reproduced, stored in a retrieval system, or transmitted in any form or by any means (electronic, mechanical, photocopying, recording, or otherwise) without written permission from Incentive Publications, Inc., with the exception below.

Pages labeled with the statement **©1995 by Incentive Publications, Inc., Nashville, TN** are intended for reproduction. Permission is hereby granted to the purchaser of one copy of LANGUAGE ARTS FOLDER FUN to reproduce these pages in sufficient quantities for meeting the purchaser's own classroom needs.

PRINTED IN THE UNITED STATES OF AMERICA

Table of Contents

INTRODUCTION

Language Arts Folder Fun was designed to assist teachers in the creation of easy-to-use materials that students will find fun and motivating. These folders lend themselves to many classroom needs: reteaching, reinforcing, enriching, extending concepts, and using as center materials or for cooperative group learning work. They also provide students with a non-threatening format in which basic language arts concepts are developed. Plus, each activity is self-checking for immediate reinforcement.

The folders are simple to construct: all elements needed to create each folder are included on a two-page spread. The first page contains the illustration to be placed on the outside of the folder. The second page presents detailed directions for creating the folder; a word bank of vocabulary words to be used in the activity (teachers may modify this list to suit their classroom needs); a word card pattern (if applicable to the activity); and an illustration showing how the folder should look upon completion.

It is recommended that teachers laminate each folder before allowing students to use it. When making folders that incorporate the use of magnetic tape, laminate the folder *first*, and then attach the tape. Folders that require holes in the word cards should have the holes punched before lamination and then re-punched after lamination.

MATERIALS NEEDED

- Manila or colored file folders
- Colored tagboard or construction paper
- Rubber cement or glue stick
- Colored markers
- Card pockets (as found in library books) or envelopes
- Assorted colors of unlined index cards
- Magnetic tape
- Paper clips
- Scissors
- Hole punch

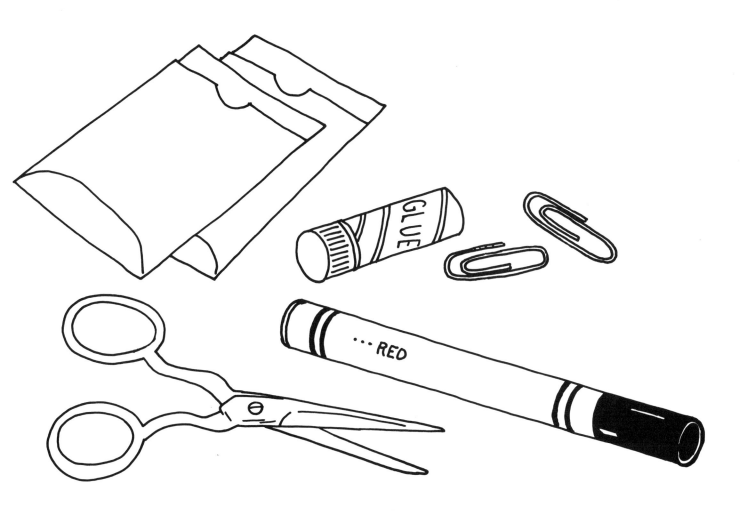

THE LONG AND SHORT OF IT

 ©1995 by Incentive Publications, Inc., Nashville, TN.

THE LONG AND SHORT OF IT

DIRECTIONS

Duplicate the cover pattern (page 8) using green construction paper or tagboard for the tree top and brown for the trunk. Cut out and glue on the front of a manila folder. Use the pattern below to make the word cards from red construction paper or tagboard. Duplicate two more trees from the cover pattern for use inside the folder. Print LONG down one tree trunk and SHORT down the other. Cut magnetic tape into small squares, and glue the squares on the tree tops. Print words from the word bank on each word card. Punch a staple through each word card, or attach a paper clip to each so that the card will adhere to the magnetic tape on the tree tops. Print directions for folder use along the bottom of the folder. Place the word cards in a 9½" x 6½" manila envelope, and attach the envelope to the inside of the folder with a paper clip. Glue a card pocket on the back of the folder. Write the answers on an index card to be placed in this pocket for self-checking.

WORD BANK

LONG

float	rice
time	clay
fume	grow
line	real
steep	moan
place	spoke
rain	queen
plate	mute
cube	pleat

SHORT

skip	hand
quilt	plot
blink	shock
clock	hedge
shut	health
prim	much
glass	plump
trust	stomp
blast	trend

WORD CARDS

float

LONG

Directions. Place the word cards with words that have long vowels on the long vowel tree, and the word cards with

SHORT

words that have short vowels on the short vowel tree. Check your answers on the back of the folder.

INSIDE

THE LONG AND SHORT OF IT

OUTSIDE

9

G-R-R-REAT SOUNDS OF "G"

 ©1995 by Incentive Publications, Inc., Nashville, TN.

G-R-R-REAT SOUNDS OF "G"

DIRECTIONS

Duplicate the cover pattern (page 10) using manila tagboard or construction paper. Color, cut out, and glue on the front of a manila folder. Make word cards from pieces of tagboard or index cards. Print a word from the word bank on each word card. Glue two card pockets on the inside of the folder. Print HARD G on one and SOFT G on the other. Print the directions for folder use on the inside of the folder. Place word cards in a 9½" x 6½" manila envelope, and attach the envelope to the inside of the folder with a paper clip. Glue a card pocket on the back of the folder. Print the answers on an index card to be placed in this pocket for self-checking.

WORD BANK

HARD G		SOFT G	
gum	gold	gem	gentle
pig	flag	giraffe	huge
ghost	girl	page	genie
twig	good	bridge	giant
garden	tag	age	fringe
gone	gate	stage	range
goat	goose	tinge	general

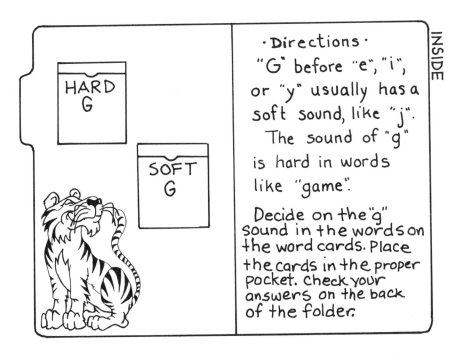

· Directions ·
"G" before "e", "i", or "y" usually has a soft sound, like "j".
The sound of "g" is hard in words like "game".

Decide on the "g" sound in the words on the word cards. Place the cards in the proper pocket. Check your answers on the back of the folder.

INSIDE

G-R-R-REAT SOUNDS OF "G"

OUTSIDE

S-H-H! SILENT LETTERS

 ©1995 by Incentive Publications, Inc., Nashville, TN.

S-H-H! SILENT LETTERS

DIRECTIONS

Duplicate the cover pattern (page 12) using manila tagboard or construction paper. Color, cut out, and glue on the front of a manila folder. Use the word card pattern below to make word cards from yellow construction paper or tagboard. Print a word from the word bank on each word card. Place the word cards in a 9½" x 6½" manila envelope, and attach the envelope to the inside of the folder with a paper clip. Print the directions for folder use on the inside of the folder. Glue a card pocket on the back of the folder. Print the answers on an index card to be placed in this pocket for self-checking.

WORD BANK

knowledge	gnaw
gnarled	knock
science	gnome
bewitch	catch
know	head

WORD CARDS

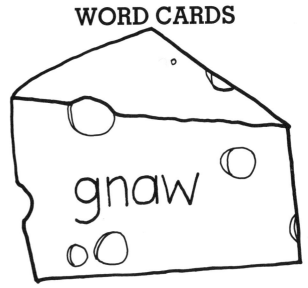

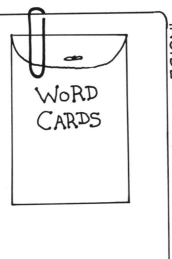

DIRECTIONS

Each word card contains a word with <u>one</u> or <u>more</u> silent letters. Slide a paper clip over the silent letters.

Check your answers on the back of the folder.

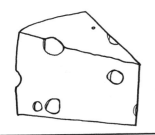

WORD CARDS

INSIDE

S-H-H! SILENT LETTERS

OUTSIDE

TALK ABOUT "C"

 ©1995 by Incentive Publications, Inc., Nashville, TN.

TALK ABOUT "C"

DIRECTIONS

Duplicate the cover pattern (page 14) using manila tagboard or construction paper. Color, cut out, and glue on the front of a manila folder. Make word cards from tagboard or index cards. On each word card, print a word from the word bank below. Glue two card pockets to the inside of the folder. Label the pockets SOFT C and HARD C. Place the word cards in a 9½" x 6½" manila envelope, and attach the envelope to the inside of the folder with a paper clip. Print directions for folder use on the inside of the folder. Glue a card pocket on the back of the folder. Print the answers on an index card to be placed in this pocket for self-checking.

WORD BANK

HARD C		SOFT C	
carrot	magic	palace	grocery
cream	arithmetic	cent	cemetery
copy	core	cereal	certain
corn	cottage	voice	notice
canoe	atomic	circus	since
second	attic	rice	race
contain	calf	center	pencil
circus			

SOFT C   HARD C

· Directions ·
When the letter "C" comes before "e", "i", and "y" it has the soft sound of "S." Otherwise, "C" has the hard sound of "K."

Place the word card in the proper pocket. Check your answers on the back of the folder.

INSIDE

TALK ABOUT "C"

OUTSIDE

15

SUNNY SOUNDS OF "Y"

©1995 by Incentive Publications, Inc., Nashville, TN.

SUNNY SOUNDS OF "Y"

DIRECTIONS

Duplicate the cover pattern (page 16) using yellow or orange tagboard or construction paper. Cut out and glue on the front of a manila folder. Make word cards from tagboard or index cards. Print a word from the word bank on each word card. Glue three card pockets on the inside of the folder. On each pocket, print LONG E, LONG I, or SHORT I. Place the word cards in a 9½" x 6½" manila envelope, and attach the envelope to the inside of the folder with a paper clip. Print the directions for folder use on the inside of the folder. Glue a card pocket on the back of the folder. Print the answers on an index card to be placed in this pocket for self-checking.

WORD BANK

LONG I		LONG E		SHORT I	
eye	my	surrey	empty	syrup	gypsy
lying	dye	somebody	sadly	cymbal	cyst
type	rhyme	baby	putty	crystal	gym
nylon	cry	glossy	jury	tryst	bicycle
why	fly	pity	taffy		
cycle	trying	ivy	rusty		
deny	spy	sticky	pretty		

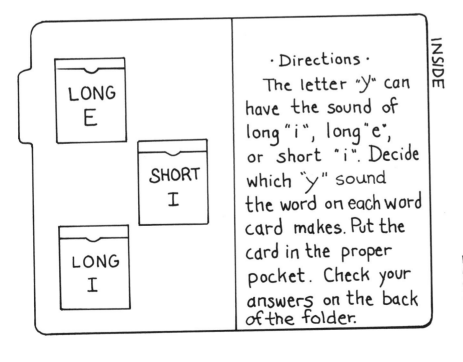

· Directions ·
The letter "y" can have the sound of long "i", long "e", or short "i". Decide which "y" sound the word on each word card makes. Put the card in the proper pocket. Check your answers on the back of the folder.

INSIDE

OUTSIDE

SUNNY SOUNDS OF "Y"

CLOWNING AROUND WITH "SH" AND "CH"

 ©1995 by Incentive Publications, Inc., Nashville, TN.

CLOWNING AROUND WITH "SH" AND "CH"

DIRECTIONS

Duplicate the cover pattern (page 18) using manila tagboard or construction paper. Color, cut out, and glue on the front of a manila folder. Using the word card pattern below, make hats from construction paper or tagboard. Print a word from the word bank on each hat, omitting the "sh" or "ch" that occurs in each word. Below the word, print "sh" on one side of the hat and "ch" on the other. Punch a hole above each (see illustration). On the back of the word card, lightly circle the correct answer with a pencil, pen, or highlighting pen so that the circle does NOT show through the front of the card. Place the word cards in a 9½" x 6½" manila envelope, and attach the envelope to the inside of the folder with a paper clip. Print the directions for folder use on the inside of the folder.

WORD BANK

SH		CH	
__ell	bru__	__ase	ri__
__are	ca__	bun__	__at
cra__	__ame	mat__	__oke
__ot	__iver	__oose	lun__
__oe	__ake	tea__er	bat__
fi__	__ine	wit__	__eat
tra__	ma__	__icken	__ain

WORD CARDS

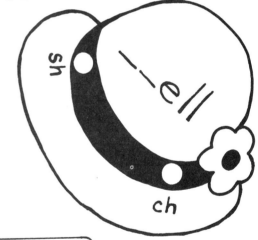

· Directions ·
   The word on each word card is missing two letters. Indicate that the missing letters are "sh" or "ch" by placing the point of your pencil in the hole above the correct letter combination. Turn the word card over. The correct answer is circled.

WORD CARDS

INSIDE

CLOWNING AROUND WITH "SH" AND "CH"

OUTSIDE

19

TIME TO RHYME

 ©1995 by Incentive Publications, Inc., Nashville, TN.

TIME TO RHYME

DIRECTIONS

Duplicate the cover pattern (page 20) using construction paper or tagboard. Color, cut out, and glue on the front of a manila folder. Use cards of two different colors for the word cards (for example, blue and white). Write the words from the word bank below on the appropriate cards. Place the word cards in a 9½" x 6½" manila envelope, and attach it to the inside of the folder with a paper clip. Print the directions for folder use on the inside of the folder. Glue a card pocket on the back of the folder. Print the answers on an index card to be placed in this pocket for self-checking.

WORD BANK

BLUE CARDS		WHITE CARDS	
hums	blow	comes	toe
wear	talk	dare	hawk
near	spool	deer	rule
steak	sheet	make	wheat
were	freeze	her	please
should	sky	wood	high
kite	head	sight	said
shoe	noise	blue	boys
rain	sour	pane	power
boot	call	flute	haul

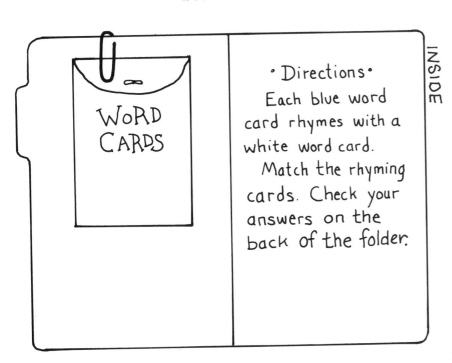

·Directions·
Each blue word card rhymes with a white word card.
Match the rhyming cards. Check your answers on the back of the folder.

WORD CARDS

INSIDE

OUTSIDE

TIME TO RHYME

DON'T MONKEY AROUND
WITH "OI" AND "OY"

©1995 by Incentive Publications, Inc., Nashville, TN.

DON'T MONKEY AROUND WITH "OI" AND "OY"

DIRECTIONS

Duplicate the cover pattern (page 22) using manila tagboard or construction paper. Color, cut out, and glue on the front of a manila folder. Using the word card pattern below, make word cards from yellow construction paper or tagboard. Print a word from the word bank on each banana, leaving two blanks where the "oi" or "oy" diphthongs should be. Glue two card pockets on the inside of the folder. Print OI on one pocket and OY on the other. Print the directions for folder use on the inside of the folder. Place the word cards in a 9½" x 6½" manila envelope, and attach the envelope to the inside of the folder with a paper clip. Glue a card pocket on the back of the folder. Print the answers on an index card to be placed inside this pocket for self-checking.

WORD BANK

OY		OI	
empl__	ann__	sp__l	p__nt
r__al	l__al	n__se	__l
__ster	destr__	s__l	ch__ce
b__	j__	c__n	br__l
enj__	t__	j__nt	c__l

WORD CARDS

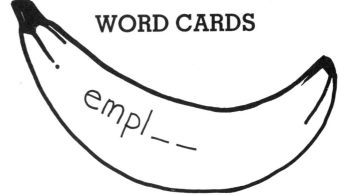

empl_ _

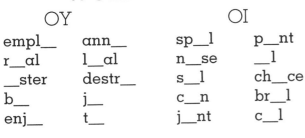

·Directions·
Decide if "oi" or "oy" should go in the blank on each word card.
Check your answers on the back of the folder.

OI OY

INSIDE

WORD CARDS

OUTSIDE

DON'T MONKEY AROUND WITH "OI" AND "OY"

"SEAL"-ECT
"OU" OR "OW"

 ©1995 by Incentive Publications, Inc., Nashville, TN.

"SEAL"-ECT "OU" OR "OW"

DIRECTIONS

Duplicate the cover pattern (page 24) using gray tagboard or construction paper. Cut out and glue on the front of a manila folder. Using the word card pattern below, make word cards from tagboard or construction paper. Print a word from the word bank on each word card, leaving two blanks in each word where "ou" or "ow" should be. Punch a hole on each side of the seal at the bottom. Above the holes, print OU or OW (see illustration). On the back of the word card, lightly circle the correct answer with a pencil, pen, or highlighting pen so that the circle does NOT show through the front of the card. Students can turn over the word cards to self-check their answers. Place the word cards in a 9½" x 6½" manila envelope, and attach the envelope to the inside of the folder. Print the directions for folder use on the inside of the folder.

WORD BANK

WORD CARDS

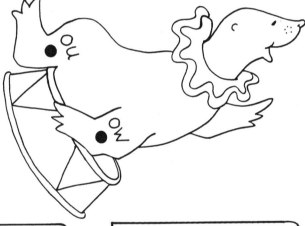

	OU		OW
m__ntain	h__se	cl__n	v__el
c__nt	r__nd	n__	d__n
__t	m__th	dr__n	br__n
m__se	sc__t	cr__n	t__n
sh__t	s__th	pl__	gr__l
		cr__d	__l

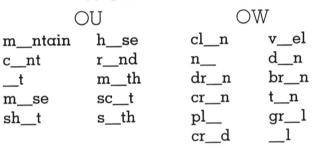
· Directions ·
On each word card, there are missing letters. Decide if the missing letters are "ou" or "ow." Place the point of your pencil in the proper hole. Turn the word card over. The correct answer is circled.

WORD CARDS

INSIDE

OUTSIDE

"SEAL"-ECT "OU" OR "OW"

25

SNAP UP SYLLABLES

 ©1995 by Incentive Publications, Inc., Nashville, TN.

SNAP UP SYLLABLES

DIRECTIONS

Duplicate the cover pattern (page 26) using manila tagboard or construction paper. Color, cut out, and glue on the front of a manila folder. Glue three card pockets on the inside of the folder. Label the pockets "1", "2", and "3." Make word cards from index cards or tagboard. Print a word from the word bank on each word card. Place the word cards in a 9½" x 6½" manila envelope, and attach the envelope to the inside of the folder with a paper clip. Print the directions for folder use on the inside of the folder. Glue a card pocket on the back of the folder. Write the answers on an index card to be placed in this pocket for self-checking.

WORD BANK

1 SYLLABLE		2 SYLLABLES		3 SYLLABLES	
pulse	leaves	science	icy	factory	oxygen
ground	friends	garage	open	classify	different
closed	stripes	photo	colonel	hospital	kangaroo
timed	chain	cabbage	fountain	bicycle	evening

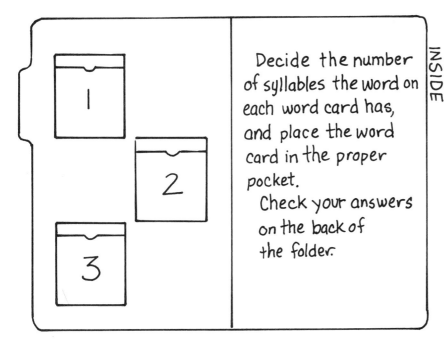

Decide the number of syllables the word on each word card has, and place the word card in the proper pocket.

Check your answers on the back of the folder.

INSIDE

SNAP UP SYLLABLES

OUTSIDE

PURRRFECT ACCENTS

28 ©1995 by Incentive Publications, Inc., Nashville, TN.

PURRRFECT ACCENTS

DIRECTIONS

Duplicate the cover pattern (page 28) using black tagboard or black construction paper. Use "white-out" (liquid correction fluid) to make the eyes and whiskers, and for outlining any other of the cat's features. Cut out this pattern, and glue it on the front of a manila folder. On the inside of the folder, glue two card pockets. Label the pockets "1" and "2." Make word cards from index cards or tagboard. Print a word from the word bank below on each word card. Be sure to divide the words into syllables on the word cards. Place the word cards in a 9½" x 6½" manila envelope, and attach the envelope to the inside of the folder with a paper clip. Print the directions for folder use on the inside of the folder. Glue a card pocket on the back of the folder. Print the answers on an index card to be placed in this pocket for self-checking.

WORD BANK

1		2	
of ten	han dle	re main der	un kind
pen cil	af ter	post pone	con di tion
lad der	na ture	a gree	pre dic tion
un cle	sta tion	fan tas tic	con fuse
love ly	fin ish	re move	ar rive
vis it	rat tle	con fess	with draw
scis sors	ba con	ac count	for get ful

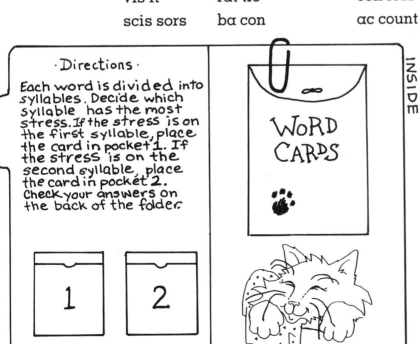

· Directions ·

Each word is divided into syllables. Decide which syllable has the most stress. If the stress is on the first syllable, place the card in pocket 1. If the stress is on the second syllable, place the card in pocket 2. Check your answers on the back of the folder.

1   2

WORD CARDS

INSIDE

PURRRFECT ACCENTS

OUTSIDE

29

FIRED UP ABOUT NOUNS AND VERBS

 ©1995 by Incentive Publications, Inc., Nashville, TN.

FIRED UP ABOUT NOUNS AND VERBS

DIRECTIONS

Duplicate the cover pattern (page 30) using construction paper or tagboard. Color, cut out, and glue on the front of a manila folder. Make sentence strips from tagboard or index cards. Write a sentence from the word bank below on each sentence strip, underlining the proper word. Print the directions for folder use on the inside of the folder. Glue two card pockets on the inside of the folder. Print NOUNS on one pocket and VERBS on the other. Place the sentence strips in a 9½" x 6½" manila envelope, and attach the envelope to the inside of the folder with a paper clip. Glue a card pocket on the back of the folder. Print the answers on an index card to be placed in this pocket for self-checking.

WORD BANK

NOUNS

George found a beautiful <u>rock</u>.
My <u>wish</u> was for a new puppy.
Max was hurt in the <u>crash</u>.
The <u>banks</u> of the river were slippery.
Mary bought a <u>scoop</u> of ice-cream for her mother.
Our <u>nurse</u> takes good care of us all.
The man hit our car and made a <u>dent</u> in it.
Andrew's <u>dream</u> was to be a doctor.
Sarah's father wore a suit and a <u>tie</u>.
A loud <u>sound</u> came from the radio.
The prize was a golden <u>ring</u>.
The <u>rake</u> at the hardware store is expensive.
We enjoyed the <u>play</u> given at the high school.

VERBS

I watched my grandmother <u>rock</u> back and forth.
Sally likes to <u>wish</u> on a star.
If he isn't careful, the car will <u>crash</u>.
Father <u>banks</u> at the First National Bank.
Johnny will <u>scoop</u> ice cream from the container.
When I am sick, my mother helps <u>nurse</u> me.
Be careful or you will <u>dent</u> the car.
Do you ever <u>dream</u> in color?
Janey will <u>tie</u> the bow on the package.
Matt can <u>sound</u> out new words well.
The church bells will <u>ring</u> at noon.
<u>Rake</u> all the leaves into a pile.
You must <u>play</u> together without fighting.

·Directions·
 A <u>noun</u> is the name of a person, place or thing.
 A <u>verb</u> is an action word.
Indicate that the underlined word is a noun or a verb by placing the sentence strip in the proper pocket. Check your answers on the back of the folder.

INSIDE

OUTSIDE

FIRED UP ABOUT NOUNS AND VERBS

GOOD LUCK WITH PLURALS

32   ©1995 by Incentive Publications, Inc., Nashville, TN.

GOOD LUCK WITH PLURALS

DIRECTIONS

Duplicate the cover pattern (page 32) using bright green construction paper or tagboard. Cut out the pattern and glue it on the front of a manila folder. Print the directions for folder use on the inside of the folder. Using the shamrock pattern below, make word cards from green construction paper. Punch a hole in each shamrock leaf. Below each hole, print "s", "es", or "ies" (see illustration below). Print one word from the word bank on each shamrock. On the back of the shamrock, lightly circle the correct answer hole with a pencil, pen, or highlighting pen so that the circle does NOT show through the front of the card. Place the shamrock word cards in a 9½" x 6½" manila envelope, and attach the envelope to the inside of the folder with a paper clip.

WORD BANK

"S"	"ES"	"IES"
fence	beach	baby
egg	grass	candy
chicken	witch	fairy
flower	fox	lady
monkey	church	berry
floor	dress	melody
clock	ax	penny
road	bunch	cherry
day	guess	party
block	circus	nanny

WORD CARDS

·Directions·

Most nouns form their plurals by adding "s" to the singular form of the word. If a noun ends in "sh","s","ch", or "x", "es" is added to the singular. If a noun ends in "y" preceeded by a consonant, the "y" is changed to "i" and "es" is added. Put the point of a pencil in the hole showing the correct plural

WORD CARDS

form of the noun on the word card. Turn the word card over to check your answer. The correct hole is circled.

INSIDE

GOOD LUCK WITH PLURALS

OUTSIDE

33

CONTRACTION CUPCAKES

 ©1995 by Incentive Publications, Inc., Nashville, TN.

CONTRACTION CUPCAKES

DIRECTIONS

Duplicate the cover pattern (page 34) using manila tagboard or construction paper. Color, cut out, and glue on the front of a manila folder. Using the word card pattern below, make cupcakes from various colors of construction paper or tagboard. Cut the tops of the cupcakes from the bottoms for matching purposes. Print the contractions from the word bank on the tops of the cupcakes and the words for which the contractions stand on the bottoms. Students will match the cupcakes. Place the cupcake parts inside a 9½" x 6½" manila envelope, and attach the envelope to the inside of the folder with a paper clip. Print the directions for folder use on the inside of the folder. Glue a card pocket on the back of the folder. Print the answers on an index card to be placed in this pocket for self-checking.

WORD BANK

it's	it is	can't	cannot
you're	you are	weren't	were not
who's	who is	there's	there is
mustn't	must not	didn't	did not
won't	will not	don't	do not
couldn't	could not	I'm	I am
they're	they are	could've	could have
we'll	we will	might've	might have
there'll	there will	isn't	is not

WORD CARDS

you're / you are — cut

·Directions·

Two words combined and using an apostrophe for an omitted letter or letters is a contraction. Match the contractions (cupcake tops) with the words they represent (cupcake bottoms). Check your answers on the back of the folder.

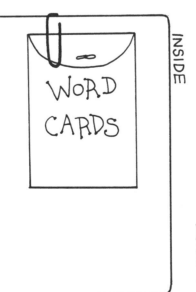

WORD CARDS

INSIDE

CONTRACTION CUPCAKES

OUTSIDE

ADVERB OR ADJECTIVE

©1995 by Incentive Publications, Inc., Nashville, TN.

ADVERB OR ADJECTIVE

DIRECTIONS

Duplicate the cover pattern (page 36) using manila tagboard or construction paper. Color, cut out, and glue on the front of a manila folder. Glue two card pockets on the inside of the folder. On one pocket, print ADJECTIVES. On the other, print ADVERBS. Make sentence strips from tagboard or index cards. Write a sentence from the word bank below on each strip, underlining the appropriate word. Place sentence strips in a 9½" x 6½" manila envelope, and attach the envelope to the inside of the folder with a paper clip. Print the directions for folder use on the inside of the folder. Glue a card pocket on the back of the folder. Print the answers on an index card to be placed in this pocket for self-checking.

WORD BANK

ADVERBS

We walked <u>quickly</u> to the park.
My homework is due <u>tomorrow</u>.
Elizabeth and I went <u>there</u> for lunch.
He drove <u>slowly</u> around the block.
Andrew does <u>well</u> in school.
Mail the letter <u>promptly</u>.
"I want the book <u>now</u>," said Sarah.
The woman looked <u>angrily</u> at the spilled milk.
<u>Suddenly</u>, a black cat appeared.
<u>Sometimes</u> the weather is warm in March.

ADJECTIVES

The <u>quick</u> fox escaped capture.
A <u>slow</u> train arrived at the station.
My <u>prompt</u> reply made the teacher happy.
Steven is an <u>angry</u> child.
The <u>sudden</u> cloudburst drenched the people.
<u>Good</u> children are always welcome.
The <u>lovely</u> rose had a sweet fragrance.
<u>Friendly</u> faces appeared at the windows.
Megan liked the <u>kindly</u> old man.
The <u>funny</u> clowns did lots of tricks at the circus.

· Directions ·
Adjectives describe nouns and pronouns. Adverbs describe verbs, adjectives, and other adverbs.
Indicate that the underlined word is an adjective or an adverb by putting the sentence strip in the proper pocket. Check your answers on the back of the folder.

INSIDE

ADVERB OR ADJECTIVE

OUTSIDE

PREFIX PIZZA

un-

dis-

re-

 ©1995 by Incentive Publications, Inc., Nashville, TN.

PREFIX PIZZA

DIRECTIONS

Duplicate the cover pattern (page 38) using manila tagboard or construction paper for the outer crust of the pizza and the three missing pieces. Use red tagboard or construction paper for the pizza toppings. Decorate the pizza (see pattern, page 38). Print RE- DIS-, and UN- on the missing slices. Glue the pizza on the outside of a manila folder. Glue three card pockets inside the folder. Print RE-, DIS-, and UN- on each pocket. Duplicate pizza slices from the word card pattern below, and print a word from the word bank on each card. Place the word cards in a 9½" x 6½" manila envelope, and attach the envelope to the inside of the folder with a paper clip. Glue a card pocket on the back of the folder. Write answers on an index card to be placed in pocket for self-checking.

WORD BANK

RE-

spell	write
view	paint
turn	plant
check	new
read	pay

DIS-

continue	lodge
honest	taste
please	agree
respect	trust
belief	obey

UN-

known	safe
kind	comfortable
easy	even
happy	fair
selfish	interesting

WORD CARDS

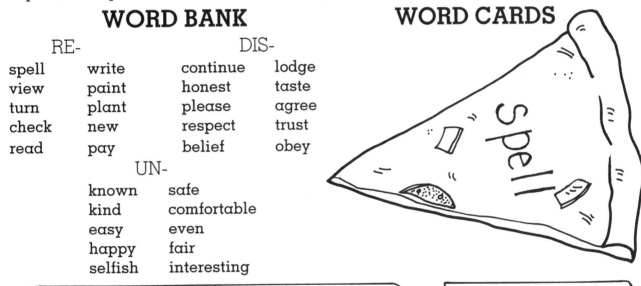

·Directions·
A prefix is a group of letters that, when placed before a word, changes the meaning of the word.

Place the word cards in the proper pocket. Check your answers on the back of the folder.

INSIDE

PREFIX PIZZA

OUTSIDE

39

A WHALE OF A SUFFIX

 ©1995 by Incentive Publications, Inc., Nashville, TN.

A WHALE OF A SUFFIX

DIRECTIONS

Duplicate the cover pattern (page 40) using manila tagboard or construction paper. Color, cut out, and glue on the front of manila folder. Glue three card pockets on the inside of the folder. Label the pockets -FUL, -ABLE, and -NESS. Make word cards from index cards or manila tagboard. Print a root word from the word bank on each word card. Place the word cards in a 9½" x 6½" manila envelope, and attach the envelope to the inside of the folder with a paper clip. Print the directions for folder use on the inside of the folder. Glue a card pocket on the back of the folder. Print the answers on an index card to be placed inside this pocket for self-checking.

WORD BANK

-FUL		-NESS		-ABLE	
help	play	light	happy	wash	erase
pain	joy	still	white	comfort	laugh
color	cheer	soft	bright	work	read
doubt	care	neat	dark	accept	wear
power	thought	kind	busy	live	depend
wonder	peace	sick	hard	break	love

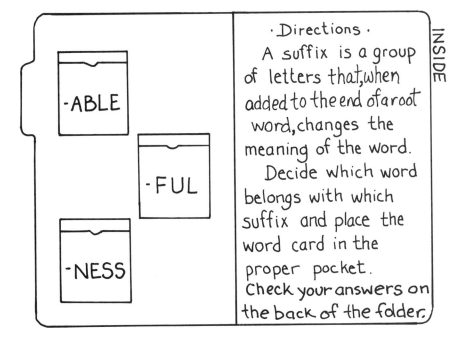

· Directions ·
A suffix is a group of letters that, when added to the end of a root word, changes the meaning of the word.
Decide which word belongs with which suffix and place the word card in the proper pocket. Check your answers on the back of the folder.

INSIDE

A WHALE OF A SUFFIX

OUTSIDE

GARDEN OF "NYMS"

GARDEN of "NYMS"

 ©1995 by Incentive Publications, Inc., Nashville, TN.

GARDEN OF "NYMS"

DIRECTIONS

Duplicate the cover pattern (page 42) using tagboard or construction paper. Color the leaf and stem green. Glue the pattern on the front of a manila folder. Duplicate two more flowers and color appropriately. Cut out the flowers, and glue one on each side of the inside of the folder. Print SYNONYM in the center of one flower and ANTONYM in the center of the other. Print one word from each synonym pair on the petals of the synonym flower and one word from each antonym pair on the petals of the antonym flower. Cut small pieces of magnetic tape and glue on each petal (see illustration). Make petal pattern word cards from tagboard or construction paper. Write corresponding synonyms and antonyms on the word cards. Attach a paper clip to each word card. Place cards in a 9½" x 6½" manila envelope, and attach the envelope to the inside of the folder with a paper clip. Write the directions for folder use on the bottom of the folder. Glue a card pocket on the back of the folder. Print the answers on an index card to be placed inside this pocket for self-checking.

WORD BANK

ANTONYMS

sick - healthy	easy - hard
day - night	better - worse
noisy - quiet	come - go
young - old	start - stop
right - wrong	big - little
cold - hot	lose - win
few - many	

SYNONYMS

cry - weep	tardy - late
gift - present	happy - elated
angry - irate	start - begin
sad - pensive	run - sprint
nice - pleasant	afraid - frightened
bad - naughty	delicious - tasty
easy - simple	end - conclude

WORD CARDS

INSIDE

OUTSIDE

irections.
Synonyms are words
hat mean almost the
same. Antonyms are
words with opposite
meanings. Match the
words on the petals

with their corresponding
word cards (either
antonym or synonym).
The paper clips will
make the petals
stay on the flowers.

GARDEN OF "NYMS"

GARDEN of "NYMS"

"NOTE" THESE HOMONYMS

©1995 by Incentive Publications, Inc., Nashville, TN.

"NOTE" THESE HOMONYMS

DIRECTIONS

Duplicate the cover pattern (page 44) using manila tagboard or construction paper. Color, cut out, and glue on the outside of a manila folder. Print directions for folder use on one side of the folder. Glue two card pockets on the other side. Print A on one pocket and B on the other. Make sentence strips from tagboard or index cards. Print a sentence from the word bank on each strip. Place sentences in a 9½" x 6½" manila envelope, and attach the envelope to the inside of the folder with a paper clip. Glue a card pocket on the back of the folder. Write the answers on an index card to be placed in the pocket for self-checking.

WORD BANK

POCKET A

1. They could ____ the drums.
   A. hear   B. here
3. His ____ balloon landed in the tree.
   A. blue   B. blew
5. The package was wrapped in ____ paper.
   A. plain   B. plane
7. We drove along the ____ street in the city.
   A. main   B. mane
9. Betsy ____ all the answers to the riddles.
   A. knew   B. new
11. The easter egg ____ comes in many colors.
    A. dye   B. die
13. Everyone watched the ads for a ____ on shoes.
    A. sale   B. sail
15. The baby was very ____ to her parents.
    A. dear   B. deer
17. Andy had ____ books in his hand.
    A. two   B. to
19. That box must ____ a ton.
    A. weigh   B. way
21. The best day of the ____ is Saturday.
    A. week   B. weak
23. Soon everyone will have new books ____ read.
    A. to   B. too

POCKET B

2. We could read the poem about the ____ .
   A. see   B. sea
4. Barbara ____ attend if she could.
   A. wood   B. would
6. Diane ____ the pottery contest.
   A. one   B. won
8. Greg was stung by a ____ .
   A. be   B. bee
10. Add the numbers to get the ____ .
    A. some   B. sum
12. Mrs. Smith's ____ will visit next week.
    A. sun   B. son
14. My favorite vegetable is a ____ .
    A. beat   B. beet
16. Travis ____ his bicycle after school.
    A. road   B. rode
18. We had a party ____ my brother.
    A. four   B. for
20. Please don't give me ____ much to carry.
    A. two   B. too
22. The basketball ____ played a great game.
    A. teem   B. team
24. What a ____ Grandmother told me about the old days!
    A. tail   B. tale

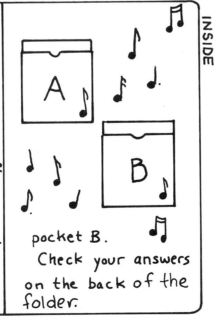

·Directions·
Words that have the same pronunciation but different spellings and meanings are called HOMONYMS.

For each sentence, choose the correct word. If your choice is A, put the sentence strip in pocket A. If your choice is B, put the sentence strip in pocket B.
Check your answers on the back of the folder.

INSIDE

"NOTE" THESE HOMONYMS

OUTSIDE

45

PUNCTUATION PARTY

 ©1995 by Incentive Publications, Inc., Nashville, TN.

PUNCTUATION PARTY

DIRECTIONS

Duplicate the cover pattern (page 46) using manila tagboard or construction paper. Color, cut out, and glue on the front of a manila folder. Make sentence strips from tagboard or index cards. On each sentence strip, print a sentence from the word bank, omitting the end punctuation mark. Glue three card pockets on the inside of the folder. Label the pockets with a large period, a question mark, and an exclamation mark. Print the directions for folder use on the inside of the folder. Place the sentence strips in a 9½" x 6½" manila envelope, and attach the envelope to the inside of the folder with a paper clip. Glue a card pocket on the back of the folder. Print the answers on an index card to be placed in this pocket for self-checking.

WORD BANK

QUESTION MARKS
Did the patriots plan the riot
Isn't it unusual to have such
    cold weather
Are you ready to go
When did the bell ring
Is it necessary to pay in
    advance
Who's going to do the dishes
Can you help at the party
Where is the elevator

EXCLAMATION MARKS
I cannot believe it
How beautiful
The house is on fire
Get out immediately
Halt
Stop running in this house
Be careful
Surprise

PERIODS
Let's change the rules
The kind policeman helped
    the old man
The air is thick with pollution
Frank listened to the radio
    each day
The accident happened at 10:00
I accepted the invitation
She sang the opera beautifully
Promptly at 7:00, the alarm rang

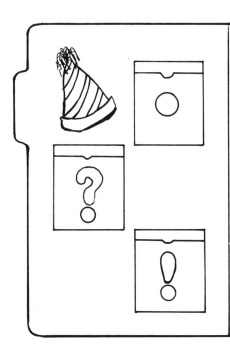

Directions
    Use a period at the end of a declarative sentence.
    Use a question mark at the end of an interrogative sentence.
    Use an exclamation mark at the end of an exclamatory sentence.
    Put the sentences in the pocket that has the needed punctuation. Check your answers on the back of the folder.

INSIDE

OUTSIDE

PUNCTUATION PARTY

BEYOND COMPARE

 ©1995 by Incentive Publications, Inc., Nashville, TN.

BEYOND COMPARE

DIRECTIONS

Duplicate the cover pattern (page 48) using manila tagboard or construction paper. Color, cut out, and glue on the front of a manila folder. Make sentence strips from manila tagboard or index cards. Print a sentence from the word bank on each sentence strip. Print the directions for folder use on the inside of the folder. Glue two card pockets on the inside of the folder. Print SIMILES on one pocket and METAPHORS on the other. Place the strips in a 9½" x 6½" manila envelope, and attach the envelope to the inside of the folder with a paper clip. Glue a card pocket on the back of the folder. Print the answers on an index card to be placed in this pocket for self-checking.

WORD BANK

SIMILES

The buffalos sounded like thunder.
The snow looks like popcorn blowing about.
The moon was as shiny as a silver coin.
The football team ate like horses.
The burglar was as quiet as a mouse.
Walter is as slow as a snail.
Sherry hurried like a hamster to the party.
The newspaper presses roared like ferocious beasts.
The overgrown yard was as wild as a jungle.
Jeremy was as proud as a peacock when he saw his grades.

METAPHORS

The fog was a thick curtain of gray.
The lawn was a green carpet.
The yellow flowers were sunshine.
The child's eyes were two big saucers when he saw the trick.
The road was a ribbon of gold in the sun.
George is a bear in the morning.
Emily is a whirlwind when it comes to cleaning.
The tree's branches were arms reaching to the sky.
The sun was a big orange hovering in the sky.
The deserted office was a tomb on weekends.
The loud classroom was a three-ring circus.

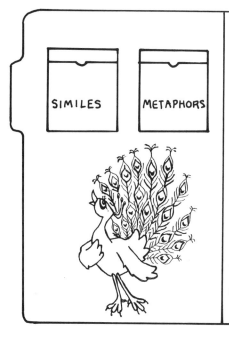

· Directions·
A <u>simile</u> compares two things using "like" or "as".
A <u>metaphor</u> compares two things by stating that one thing <u>is</u> another.
Decide if the sentence contains a simile or a metaphor. Put the strip in the proper pocket. Check your answers on the back of the folder.

SIMILES   METAPHORS

INSIDE

OUTSIDE

BEYOND COMPARE

49

CROWING ABOUT CONTEXT

 ©1995 by Incentive Publications, Inc., Nashville, TN.

CROWING ABOUT CONTEXT

DIRECTIONS

Duplicate the cover pattern (page 50) using manila tagboard or construction paper. Color, cut out, and glue on the front of a manila folder. Make sentence strips and word cards from manila tagboard or index cards. Print a sentence from the word bank on each sentence strip and a word that completes the sentence on each word card. Place the sentence strips and word cards in a 9½" x 6½" manila envelope, and attach the envelope to the inside of the folder with a paper clip. Print the directions for folder use on the inside of the folder. Glue a card pocket on the back of the folder. Print the answers on an index card to be placed in this pocket for self-checking.

WORD BANK

1. The stray dog that came to our house was
2. Matthew said, "I can carry this box. It is very
3. Kate is learning how to
4. The boat came through the storm
5. We see stars in the
6. There is smoke coming from the
7. The airplane is ready to make a
8. In autumn, the trees are
9. There is no thread on this
10. The old house was dark and
11. The poor child's coat was torn and
12. The gentleman's manners showed that he was
13. Because Patrick could not go to the park, he was
14. Lauren is afraid of many things. She is said to be
15. Bill is a hard worker. He is very

1. homeless
2. light
3. cook
4. safely
5. heavens
6. chimney
7. landing
8. leafless
9. spool
10. scary
11. tattered
12. courteous
13. disappointed
14. fearful
15. industrious

·Directions·
Each sentence strip has a word card that completes the meaning of the sentence. Match the word card with the proper sentence. Check your answers on the back of the folder.

WORD CARDS

INSIDE

OUTSIDE

CROWING ABOUT CONTEXT

WHY, WHEN, WHERE?

Why

When

Where

 ©1995 by Incentive Publications, Inc., Nashville, TN.

WHY, WHEN, WHERE?

DIRECTIONS

Duplicate the cover pattern (page 52) using manila tagboard or construction paper. Color, cut out, and glue on the front of a manila folder. Make sentence strips from tagboard or index cards. Print a phrase from the word bank on each strip. Print directions for folder use on the inside of the folder. Glue three card pockets on the inside of the folder. Print WHEN, WHY, or WHERE on each pocket. Place the sentence strips in a 9½" x 6½" manila envelope, and attach the envelope to the inside of the folder with a paper clip. Glue a card pocket on the back of the folder. Print the answers on an index card to be placed in this pocket for self-checking.

WORD BANK

WHEN	WHY	WHERE
after lunch	because I studied	on the street
until you call	if you practice	under the table
while the water boiled	since Joe is a good player	off the bridge
as soon as you can	because of the noise	into the air
before school	since it was broken	on my desk
during recess	because he was careless	in the chair
		against the wall

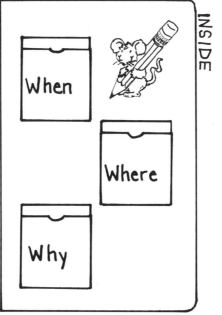

INSIDE

• Directions •
Indicate if the phrase tells you <u>when</u> something happened, <u>where</u> something happened, or <u>why</u> something happened by placing each phrase strip in the proper pocket. Check your answers on the back of the folder.

When

Where

Why

OUTSIDE

WHY, WHEN, WHERE?

Why
When
Where

DIVE INTO SEQUENCING

 ©1995 by Incentive Publications, Inc., Nashville, TN.

DIVE INTO SEQUENCING

DIRECTIONS

Duplicate the cover pattern (page 54) using manila tagboard or construction paper. Color, cut out, and glue on the front of a manila folder. Cut index cards in four colors into sentence strips. Print the sentences in the word bank that make up the stories on the sentences strips, using a single color for each story. Number the order of the sentences on the back of the strips for self-checking purposes. Print the directions for folder use on the inside of the folder. Place the sentence strips in a 9½" x 6½" manila envelope, and attach the envelope to the inside of the folder with a paper clip. Students arrange the strips in proper order to form a sensible story and check their answers by turning over the strips.

WORD BANK

1. Laura had been watching her mom knit a sweater for weeks.
2. She did not know how much time it took to make it.
3. Laura only knew that she wanted a fluffy blue sweater.
4. Laura thought her mom must be really special to take that much time for her.

1. Christopher stood looking into the bakery window for a long time.
2. He could not make up his mind which cake he wanted.
3. The one with the chocolate icing looked so good.
4. Then Christopher saw one that had nuts on its top.
5. He was ready to get it, but then he spied a better one.
6. It had strawberries and whipped cream all over it.
7. Which one do you think he got?

1. Betsy's dog Ralph knows quite a lot of tricks.
2. They are all very nice tricks, but they are unusual.
3. Ralph can turn on the television by pushing the button with his nose.
4. He also turns on the garden hose with his paw when he wants a drink.
5. Ralph has even learned to open the mailbox.
6. Betsy thinks Ralph and his tricks are wonderful. Don't you?

1. Kathy and Kristin decided to make peanut butter fudge.
2. The fudge they made was delicious, but the mess they made was awful!
3. There was sugar spilled all over the floor, and milk was splashed everywhere.
4. They had also broken two measuring cups.
5. Next time Kathy and Kristin get hungry for fudge, Mom is going to send them to the store to buy it.

•Directions•
Each group of sentences tells a story. Put the cards into color groups. Then read the sentence in each group and arrange them in order
So that they make a sensible story.
Turn the cards over to check your answers. They are numbered on the back.

WORD CARDS

INSIDE

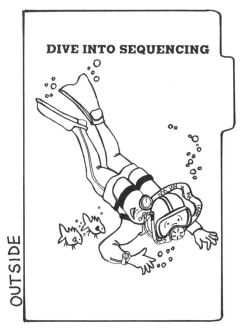

DIVE INTO SEQUENCING

OUTSIDE

WHICH CAME FIRST?

 ©1995 by Incentive Publications, Inc., Nashville, TN.

WHICH CAME FIRST?

DIRECTIONS

Duplicate the cover pattern (page 56) using manila tagboard or construction paper. Color, cut out, and glue on the front of a manila folder. Write the sentences from the word bank on strips of tagboard or index cards. Place sentence strips in a 9½" x 6½" manila envelope, and attach the envelope to the inside of the folder with a paper clip. On three card pockets, print BEFORE, AFTER, or SAME TIME, and glue the pockets on the inside of the folder. Print the directions for folder use on the inside of the folder. Glue a card pocket on the back of the folder. Print the answers on an index card to be placed in this pocket for self-checking.

WORD BANK

1. Larry bought dog food and placed it in the station wagon.
2. While the rain poured down, the wind blew violently.
3. Man flew in airplanes then flew to the moon.
4. The children hurried for shelter as the storm approached.
5. The fruit ripened and the branches grew heavier.
6. Michael found his homework where he left it the night before.
7. Define the word before you try to use it.
8. When I ran out the door, it slammed shut.
9. Sally hung up her coat and ran into the room.
10. The crowd cheered as Frank made a touchdown.
11. Sam does his homework after he gets home from school.
12. The struggle for equality started long before the Civil War.

FISHING FOR FACT
AND OPINION

 ©1995 by Incentive Publications, Inc., Nashville, TN.

FISHING FOR FACT AND OPINION

DIRECTIONS

Duplicate the cover pattern (page 58) using manila tagboard or construction paper. Color, cut out, and glue on the front of a manila folder. On the inside of the folder, glue two card pockets. Print FACT on one pocket and OPINION on the other. Cut sentence strips from index cards or manila tagboard. Write a sentence from the word bank on each sentence strip. Place the sentence strips in a 9½" x 6½" manila envelope, and attach the envelope to the inside of the folder with a paper clip. Print the directions for folder use on the inside of the folder. Glue a card pocket on the back of the folder. Print the answers on an index card to be placed in this pocket for self-checking.

WORD BANK

FACT

The sun is a star.
UP and DOWN are antonyms.
6 plus 6 equals 12.
If you mix red and yellow, you get orange.
The alphabet has 26 letters.
Plants need water to live.
There are 4 seasons in a year.
Austin is the capital of Texas.
Oak trees grow from acorns.
Olympic games are held every 4 years.

OPINION

A dog makes the best pet.
Carrots are the tastiest vegetable.
Watching T.V. is more fun than playing football.
White shoes look better than black shoes.
Apples taste better than pears.
The best job to have is that of a doctor.
Red is the best color for a car.
Fall is the nicest time of the year.
Soccer is easier to play than football.
Math is easy.

•Directions•
Facts are things that are always true and can be proved.
Opinions are things that some people believe. Indicate whether the sentences on the strips are facts

FACT   OPINION

WORD CARDS

or opinions by placing the strips in the proper pockets. Check your answers on the back of the folder.

INSIDE

FISHING FOR FACT AND OPINION

OUTSIDE

WADE THROUGH CAUSE AND EFFECT

 ©1995 by Incentive Publications, Inc., Nashville, TN.

WADE THROUGH CAUSE AND EFFECT

DIRECTIONS

Duplicate the cover pattern (page 60) using construction paper or manila tagboard. Color, cut out, and glue on the front of a manila folder. Make sets of word cards of two different colors (i.e. blue and yellow) using tagboard or index cards. Write the causes on one set of word cards and the effects on the other set. Print the directions for folder use on the inside of the folder. Place the word cards in a 9½" x 6½" manila envelope, and attach the envelope to the inside of the folder with a paper clip. Glue a card pocket on the back of the folder. Print the answers on an index card to be placed in this pocket for self-checking.

WORD BANK

CAUSES (BLUE CARDS)

Because Jack hit the ball too hard
Jim dropped the bank
The clock had stopped
Tom ran so fast that
Ellen was thirsty
Because Sally fell in the mud
When the sun came out
The child fell down
When it rained
As a result of studying so hard
Because he was so hungry
The baby was so tired
When Joe told a joke
When the strangers came
Betty ate so much candy

EFFECTS (YELLOW CARDS)

he broke a window.
so his money scattered.
so Father was late.
he became out of breath.
so she drank all the milk.
she got dirty.
the snowman melted.
and began crying.
Mother got all wet.
Suzy made a good grade.
Tom ate all of his lunch.
that she immediately fell asleep.
all the boys laughed.
my dog began barking.
that she became sick.

· Directions ·
A <u>cause</u> makes something happen.
An <u>effect</u> is what happens as a result of a cause.

Match the cause (blue card) with its effect (yellow card). Check your answers on the back of the folder.

WORD CARDS

INSIDE

WADE THROUGH CAUSE AND EFFECT

OUTSIDE

HATS OFF TO GUIDE WORDS

 ©1995 by Incentive Publications, Inc., Nashville, TN.

HATS OFF TO GUIDE WORDS

DIRECTIONS

Duplicate the cover pattern (page 62) using colored tagboard or colored construction paper. Cut out and glue on the front of a manila folder. Make word cards from tagboard or index cards. On each word card, print a word from the word bank. Glue four card pockets on the inside of the folder. On each pocket, print DOUBT–DRAB, DEPEND–DESCEND, DILIGENT–DIMITY, or DEACON–DEER. Print the directions for folder use on the inside of the folder. Place word cards in a 9½" x 6½" manila envelope, and attach the envelope to the inside of the folder with a paper clip. Glue a card pocket on the back of the folder. Print the answers on an index card to be placed in this pocket for self-checking.

WORD BANK

DILIGENT — DIMITY
- dilly
- dime
- diminish
- dill

DOUBT — DRAB
- doze
- downfall
- dough
- dove

DEPEND — DESCEND
- derrick
- depress
- derive
- depth

DEACON — DEAR
- dead
- deaf
- dean
- dealer

·Directions·

Guide words appear at the top of a dictionary page to tell you which words are on that page.

Place the word cards in the pockets which have listed matching guide words.

Check your answers on the back of the folder.

INSIDE

HATS OFF TO GUIDE WORDS

OUTSIDE

63

WHAT'S COOKIN'?

 ©1995 by Incentive Publications, Inc., Nashville, TN.

WHAT'S COOKIN'?

DIRECTIONS

Duplicate the cover pattern (page 64) using manila tagboard or construction paper. Color, cut out, and glue on the front of a manila folder. Using the word card pattern below, make rolling pins from manila tagboard or construction paper. Write a word from the word bank on each pin. Glue three card pockets on the inside of the manila folder. Print ANIMALS, FOOD, or PLANTS on each pocket. Place the word cards in a 9½" x 6½" manila envelope, and attach the envelope to the inside of the folder with a paper clip. Glue a card pocket on the back of the folder. Write the answers on an index card to be placed inside this pocket for self-checking.

WORD BANK

FOOD

spaghetti	broccoli
tangerine	zucchini
potatoes	celery
apricots	eggplant
cocoa	spinach

PLANTS

tulip	fern
violet	begonia
cactus	bluebonnet
daisy	lily
zinnia	iris

WORD CARDS

ANIMALS

walrus	cobra
panda	reindeer
moose	raven
greyhound	kangaroo
coyote	oyster

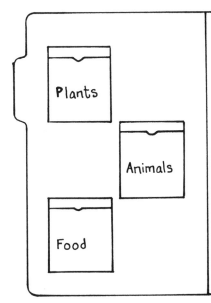

Plants

Animals

Food

Directions
Each word card is the name of an animal, a plant, or a food. Put the word card in the proper pocket. Check your answers on the back of the folder.

INSIDE

WHAT'S COOKIN'?

OUTSIDE

65

WHERE DO YOU LOOK?

 ©1995 by Incentive Publications, Inc., Nashville, TN.

WHERE DO YOU LOOK?

DIRECTIONS

Duplicate the cover pattern (page 66) using manila tagboard or construction paper. Color, cut out, and glue on the front of a manila folder. Inside the folder, glue four card pockets. Print DICTIONARY, ATLAS, ALMANAC, or ENCYCLOPEDIA on the front of each pocket. Print the directions for folder use on the inside of the folder. Print the questions from the word bank on sentence strips made from tagboard or index cards. Place cards in a 9½" x 6½" manila envelope, and attach the envelope to the inside of the folder with a paper clip. Glue a card pocket on the back of the folder. Write the answers on an index card to be placed in this pocket for self-checking.

WORD BANK

DICTIONARY

What part of speech is "magenta"?
Which syllable in the word "pelican" is stressed?
How do you pronounce "gregarious"?
How many meanings are there for the word "hitch"?
What is the root word in "indisposed"?

ATLAS

How far is it from Los Angeles to San Francisco?
Where is Algeria?
Which states border Indiana?
On what continent is Zimbabwe?
Find the shortest route between Dallas and Austin.
What states border the Great Lakes?

ENCYCLOPEDIA

When was Robert Browning born?
How does an electric motor work?
What were some of Benjamin Franklin's inventions?
Who was Amelia Earhart and what did she do?
How was penicillin discovered?

ALMANAC

What is the average rainfall in California?
What was the population of the U. S. in 1992?
Who were the top tennis players in 1989?
What is the world's longest river?

· Directions ·
Read the questions on the word card. Decide in which reference book you would find the answer. Put the word card in the proper pocket. Check your answers on the back of the folder.

ALMANAC DICTIONARY ATLAS ENCYCLO·PEDIA

INSIDE

OUTSIDE

WHERE DO YOU LOOK?

KEY WORDS

 ©1995 by Incentive Publications, Inc., Nashville, TN.

KEY WORDS

DIRECTIONS

Duplicate the cover pattern (page 68) using manila tagboard or construction paper. Color, cut out, and glue on the front of a manila folder. Using the pattern below, make word cards from construction paper or tagboard. Print a question from the word bank on each card. Below each question, print three choices for the answer. Punch a hole above each choice (see illustration). On the back of the word card, lightly circle the correct answer with pencil, pen, or high-lighting pen so that the answer does NOT show through the front. Print the directions for folder use on the inside of the folder. Place word cards in 9½" x 6½" manila envelope, and attach the envelope to inside of folder with a paper clip.

WORD BANK

1. Is the bite of a Black Widow spider deadly?
    spider   poison   black
2. Who was the first man in space?
    rockets   man   space
3. When did William Shakespeare die?
    drama   William   Shakespeare
4. Who was President during the Civil War?
    Civil   War   president
5. Which animals hibernate during winter?
    hibernate   animals   winter
6. Which fruits contain Vitamin C?
    vitamins   fruits   nutrition
7. Name three of Thomas Edison's famous inventions.
    inventions   Thomas   Edison
8. What are the primary colors?
    paint   colors   primary
9. Which famous composer was deaf?
    deaf   music   composers
10. Where is the Kentucky Derby run each year?
    Kentucky   races   Derby

WORD CARDS

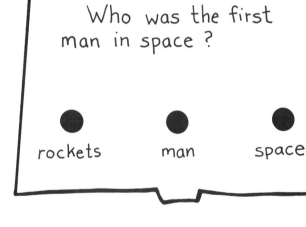

Who was the first man in space ?

rockets   man   space

•Directions•
Each word card asks for information which can be found in an encyclopedia. Decide which key word you would use to look up this information. Place a pencil point in the hole above the most correct answer. Turn the card over. The most correct answer is circled.

WORD CARDS

INSIDE

OUTSIDE

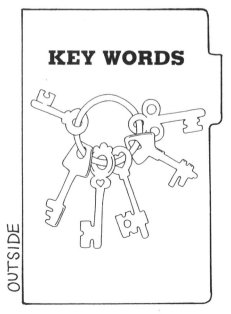

KEY WORDS

SEE THE U.S.A.

 ©1995 by Incentive Publications, Inc., Nashville, TN.

SEE THE U.S.A.

DIRECTIONS

Duplicate the cover pattern (page 70) using manila tagboard or construction paper. Color, cut out, and glue on the front of a manila folder. Duplicate the map of the United States (page 80), and glue it on the inside of the folder. On each dot on the map, glue a small square of magnetic tape. Beside each square of tape, print a letter of the alphabet. Make word cards from tagboard or index cards. On each word card, print the name of a capital city of the United States. Punch a staple through each word card or attach a paper clip to each one so that it will adhere to the magnetic tape. Print directions for folder use on the inside of the folder. Glue a card pocket on the inside of the folder beneath the directions, and place the word cards inside.

WORD BANK

Olympia, WA	Lincoln, NE	Jackson, MS	Montpelier, VT
Salem, OR	Denver, CO	Baton Rouge, LA	Concord, NH
Sacramento, CA	Topeka, KA	Lansing, MI	Albany, NY
Helena, MT	Oklahoma City, OK	Harrisburg, PA	Boston, MA
Boise, ID	Santa Fe, NM	Columbus, OH	Hartford, CT
Salt Lake City, UT	Austin, TX	Charleston, WV	Providence, RI
Carson City, NV	St. Paul, MN	Frankfort, KY	Trenton, NJ
Phoenix, AZ	Madison, WI	Nashville, TN	Dover, DE
Bismarck, ND	Indianapolis, IN	Atlanta, GA	Annapolis, MD
Pierre, SD	Springfield, IL	Montgomery, AL	Richmond, VA
Des Moines, IA	Jefferson City, MO	Tallahassee, FL	Raleigh, NC
Cheyenne, WY	Little Rock, AR	Augusta, ME	Columbia, SC
Juneau, AK	Honolulu, HI		

·Directions·
The word cards have the names of U.S. state capitals. Place each capital on the proper location. Check the classroom map for correct answers.

WORD CARDS

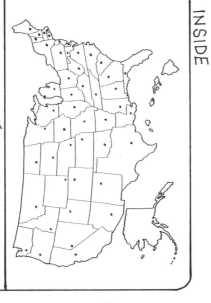

INSIDE

OUTSIDE

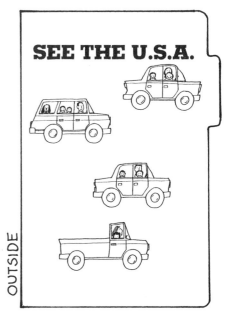

SEE THE U.S.A.

A GOOD MATCH

 ©1995 by Incentive Publications, Inc., Nashville, TN.

A GOOD MATCH

DIRECTIONS

Duplicate the cover pattern (page 72) using manila tagboard or construction paper. Color, cut out, and glue on the front of a manila folder. Make two sets of word cards from different colors of tagboard or index cards (i.e. blue and yellow). Print a word from the word bank on the each card. Print the directions for folder use on the inside of the folder. Place the word cards in a 9½" x 6½" manila envelope, and attach the envelope to the inside of the folder with a paper clip. Glue a card pocket on the back of the folder. Print the answers on an index card to be placed in this pocket for self-checking.

WORD CARDS

BLUE CARDS		YELLOW CARDS	
bag	ten	gab	net
nap	now	pan	won
lap	pin	pal	nip
tub	pot	but	top
spot	stop	tops	pots
tin	sag	nit	gas
tap	tar	pat	rat
war	was	raw	saw
ton	mug	not	gum

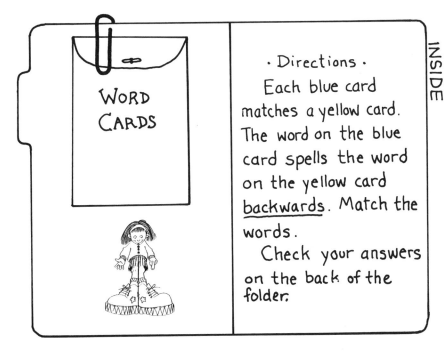

HOT DOG SPELLING

 ©1995 by Incentive Publications, Inc., Nashville, TN.

HOT DOG SPELLING

DIRECTIONS

Duplicate the cover pattern (page 74) using manila tagboard or construction paper. Color, cut out, and glue on the front of a manila folder. Use the pattern below to make word cards for the hot dogs from red construction paper and word cards for the buns from tan construction paper. Print the words from the word bank on the hot dogs and their respellings on the buns. Students will match hot dogs to buns, folding bun over hot dog at the dotted line. Place all word cards in a 9½" x 6½" manila envelope, and attach the envelope to the inside of the folder with a paper clip. Print directions for folder use on the inside of the folder. Glue a card pocket on the back of the folder. Print answers on an index card to be placed in this pocket for self-checking.

WORD BANK

soldier	sōl'jer	crescent	kres'ənt
science	sī'əns	mere	mir
chaos	kā'os	choir	kwīr
gaunt	gônt	exercise	ek'sər sīz
relieve	rəlēv'	wreck	rek
flaunt	flônt	exact	ig zakt'
czar	zär	knoll	nōl
receive	rəsēv'	honor	on'ər
knight	nīt	gnat	nat

WORD CARDS

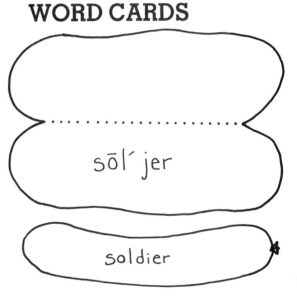

•Directions•

Match each word with its phonetic spelling. Place hot dog (word) inside bun (phonetic spelling) and fold bun over at the dotted line. Check your answers on the back of the folder.

WORD CARDS

INSIDE

OUTSIDE

HOT DOG SPELLING

TALL TALES

 ©1995 by Incentive Publications, Inc., Nashville, TN.

TALL TALES

DIRECTIONS

Duplicate the cover pattern (page 76) using manila tagboard or construction paper. Color, cut out, and glue on the front of a manila folder. Make word cards from tagboard or index card strips. On each strip, print a word from the word bank. Glue four card pockets on the inside of the folder. On each pocket, print HEROES, HARDSHIPS, HUMOR, or EXAGGERATION. Place the word cards in the proper pockets. Print directions for folder use on the inside of the folder.

WORD BANK

HEROES

Oilslick Ollie Firefightin' Fred
Seven-Foot Sue Mighty Martha
Billy Bigbrain Leo Longlegs
Arnold Astronaut Singin' Sarah
Rapid Robert Melting Man

HARDSHIPS

Lost in outer space
Cornered by a man-eating tiger
Locked in a dungeon
Fell overboard in middle of Atlantic
Wandered into crocodile-filled swamp
Trapped at bottom of well
Ate strange mushrooms and became one inch high
Sat on seat covered with instant-setting glue
Had to solve 150 math problems in 45 seconds
Roaming around in the Sahara Desert without
    a map or water

HUMOR

Sneezed and blew down a barn
Dug a hole and found himself
    in China
Used a garden spade for a
    spoon
Used plastic sandwich bags
    for galoshes
Had a pet rattlesnake for a
    belt
Started earthquakes when he
    snored
Used a pink wheelbarrow for
    transportation
Kept a potato for a pet
Had red, white, and blue
    freckles
Had a bird's nest in his beard

EXAGGERATION

Took steps 3 miles long
Could break iron bars with
    one hand
Put out fires by spitting on
    them
Ate 50 loaves of bread a day
Could sing snakes to sleep
Could solve problems faster
    than a computer
Could speak a cat's language
Had the ability to slither
    through keyholes
Had sonar ears that could
    detect any moving object
Could transform himself into
    a pencil

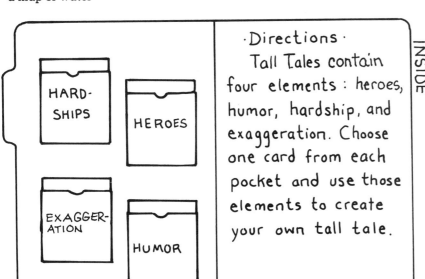

·Directions·
Tall Tales contain four elements: heroes, humor, hardship, and exaggeration. Choose one card from each pocket and use those elements to create your own tall tale.

INSIDE

OUTSIDE

77

WHO DONE IT?

 ©1995 by Incentive Publications, Inc., Nashville, TN.

WHO DONE IT?

DIRECTIONS

Duplicate the cover pattern (page 78) using manila tagboard or construction paper. Color, cut out, and glue on the front of a manila folder. Make word cards from manila tagboard or index cards. On each strip, print a word from the word bank. Glue four card pockets on the inside of the folder. On each pocket, print CHARACTERS, CLUES, CRIMES, or SUSPENSE. Place word cards in the proper pockets. Print the directions on the inside of the folder.

WORD CARDS

CHARACTERS
- Detective McIntosh
- Amanda Snoop, retired schoolteacher
- Jimmy Justice, boy wonder
- Sergeant Search
- Polly Pry, super sleuth
- Archie, the clue-sniffing cat
- Policewoman Cindy Clew
- Nosey Rosie
- Pete, the Private Eye

CLUES
- The telephone call was traced
- Fingerprints matched
- A torn piece of cloth was left behind
- Footprints were found
- Handwriting was the same
- Eyewitness identified a license plate
- A matchbook was dropped at the scene
- Tire tracks were discovered
- Part of a note was left behind
- A button turned up at the scene

CRIMES
- Top secret file is missing
- Mrs. Uppity's jewels were stolen
- Goldfish disappears from bowl
- Farmer George's barn is burned down
- Gold shipment is stolen from Frontier Bank
- Mrs. Periwinkle's purse is snatched
- Tom Malone's locker is broken into
- Mr. Peabody's prize dog is kidnapped
- A rare painting vanishes from the museum
- A secret code falls into enemy hands

SUSPENSE
- Footsteps came closer and closer
- The floor creaked
- A dog howled outside
- The door slammed shut
- An eerie stillness engulfed the room
- The doorknob slowly turned
- A cold, black secret passage emerged
- A shadowy figure appeared at the window
- The lights suddenly went out
- The telephone went dead

· Directions ·
Mystery stories contain the following elements: characters, clues, crimes, and suspense.

Choose one card from each pocket and use those elements to create your own mystery story.

Characters

Crimes

Clues

Suspense

INSIDE

WHO DONE IT?

OUTSIDE

79

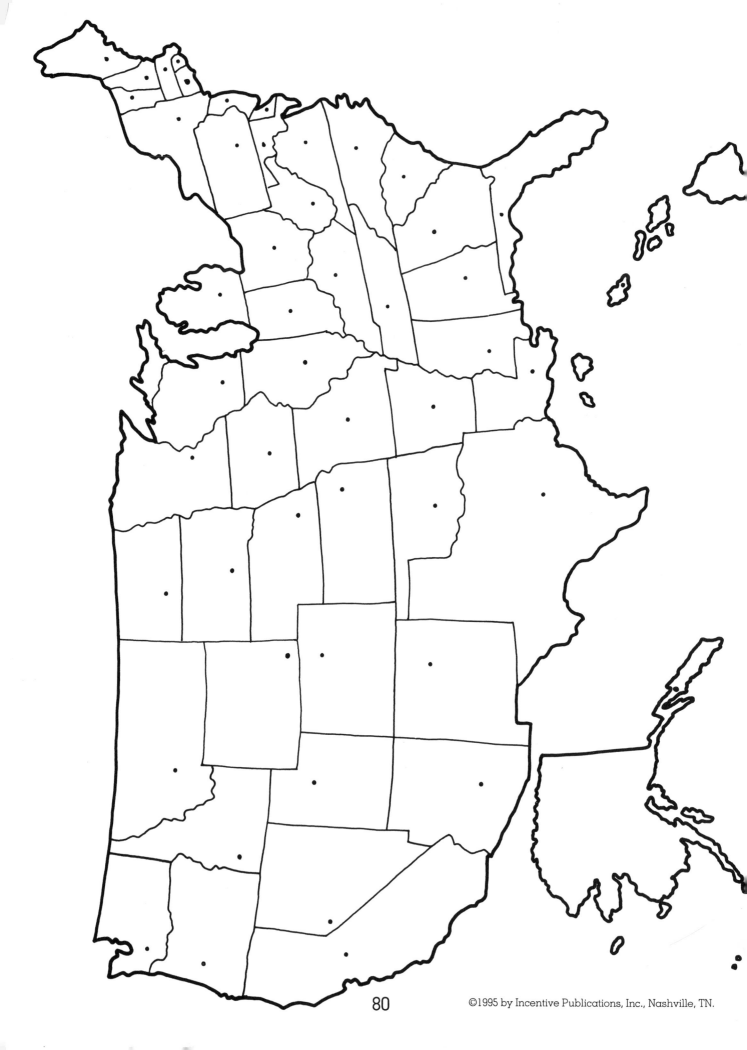

©1995 by Incentive Publications, Inc., Nashville, TN.